CITIES OF THE
WORLD

# CAPE TOWN

BY R. CONRAD STEIN

CHILDREN'S PRESS®
A Division of Grolier Publishing
New York London Hong Kong Sydney
Danbury, Connecticut

## CONSULTANTS

**Esther Fillmore**
Liaison Department
South African Consulate General, Chicago

**Linda Cornwell**
Learning Resource Consultant
Indiana Department of Education

**Project Editor:** Downing Publishing Services
**Design Director:** Karen Kohn & Associates, Ltd.
**Photo Researcher:** Jan Izzo

**Library of Congress Cataloging-in-Publication Data**
Stein, R. Conrad.
     Cape Town / by R. Conrad Stein.
         p.  cm. — (Cities of the world)
     Includes bibliographical references and index.
     Summary: Describes the history, culture, daily life, food, people, sports,
and points of interest of the legislative capital of South Africa.
     ISBN 0-516-20781-4
     1.  Cape Town (South Africa)—Juvenile literature.   [1. Cape Town (South Africa)]
I.  Title.   II.  Series: Cities of the world (New York, N.Y.)
DT2405.C364S74   1998                                             98-22246
968.7'355—dc21                                             CIP
                                AC

# TABLE OF CONTENTS

Wherever you stand outdoors in Cape Town, you will see Table Mountain. The great mountain rises 3,563 feet (1,086 meters) above the city. It is called Table Mountain because of its remarkably flat top. Viewed from city streets, the mountain's peak is so unbroken it seems to have been chiseled to table-top flatness by a giant carpenter. Clouds often swirl over Table Mountain's level crown. Such cloud formations are called its "Tablecloth."

Visitors can take a five-minute cable-car ride to the top of of Table Mountain. From the top, one looks down to see the city of Cape Town hugging the coast of the Atlantic Ocean. There are few other places on earth where mountains, the sea, and a city meet so dramatically.

Cape Town sits at the southwestern coast of the nation of South Africa. It is near the Cape of Good Hope, where the Indian Ocean meets the Atlantic Ocean. This is a strategic sea-lane location. For hundreds of years, ships from all parts of the world have stopped at Cape Town's fine port. The influx of people from various nations molded Cape Town into what it is today: one of the world's greatest multiracial and multicultural cities.

*A view of Table Mountain from Cape Town*

*The Cape of
Good Hope*

## Devil's Peak

Another lofty mountain called Devil's Peak stands just to the side of Table Mountain. It is the source of a legend known to Cape Town children. According to the legend, a pirate named Van Hunks sat on Devil's Peak and got into a pipe-smoking contest with the devil. The contest was never resolved. The pirate and the devil still inhabit Devil's Peak and continue to smoke. The legend further says it is the smoke from their pipes that creates the cloud formation called the Tablecloth.

# TOWN

South Africa has had a turbulent past. For more than three hundred years, whites fought blacks on the nation's soil. Until recently, blacks suffered under a white-dominated government that denied human rights to all nonwhites. But despite the nation's violent history, Cape Town is a happy city. People smile at one another. Flowers bloom in gardens. The sidewalks are shaded by trees. These pleasant conditions invite visitors to take walks and gather impressions of this unusual place.

# IMPRESSIONS OF THE PEOPLE

Greenmarket Square hosts one of Cape Town's lively street markets. Vendors sell everything from used shoes to expensive jewelry. Street entertainers such as puppeteers and jugglers keep the crowds amused. But just looking at the faces of Cape Towners is as entertaining as watching the street performers. Cape Town, perhaps more than any other place in the world, is a rainbow city. Gathered in the square are blacks, whites, Asians, and a mixed-race group who are called coloureds. Most of the time these rainbow people get along with one another quite well. Peace reigns in Cape Town despite terrible frictions in the past.

Not long ago, the South African government listed its citizens in four main categories: black, white, coloured, and Asian. Nearly every aspect of a citizen's life depended on the group in which the person was placed. Those who were listed as coloured had to go to a coloured school and live in a coloured section of town. Those in the black group had to go to all-black schools and live in a city section designated a black district.

*Above: Customers at Greenmarket Square might find an African teaspoon like this one for sale.*

*Right: This formerly whites-only state school was integrated in 1995.*

*Signs like this one were seen all over Cape Town and the rest of South Africa in the days of white rule.*

*Schoolchildren holding new South Africa flags celebrate the opening of Parliament.*

Whites have always been the minority group in South Africa. Today, whites make up only 17 percent of the national population. But whites were a very rich minority, owning most of the land and the businesses. The whites also ran the government. To cement their power, the whites passed laws forbidding nonwhites to enter restaurants, movie theaters, or other facilities designated for whites only. The laws created a racial pyramid. Whites were at the peak of the pyramid and other groups formed layers below them.

For years, nonwhite men and women and their white allies fought to do away with this unfair system of separating the races. Finally, they won in the long struggle. The restrictive laws ended officially in the early 1990s. In 1994, Nelson Mandela, a black man, was elected president of South Africa. Today, the nation is a democracy. Day by day, South Africa now reinvents itself as it eases into majority rule.

In Cape Town, few people appear to be bitter when discussing the old days of white rule. In one Cape Town neighborhood, faded words announcing WHITE ENTRANCE can still be seen painted over the doorway of a cleaning store. The store owner, who is Asian, shrugged his shoulders when asked about the sign. He said one of these days he'll paint the building and cover up the sign. Like the sign, the old system is a fading memory in modern Cape Town.

*The multiracial community of Wynberg holds an annual carnival that features ethnic merchandise and food.*

# CELEBRATING DIVERSITY

White. Black. Asian. Coloured. Those one-word labels once ruled a South African's life from birth to death. In terms of the law, racial categories mean nothing today. Yet people still identify with their racial groups. Habits of a lifetime do not change overnight. In Cape Town, the most ethnically diverse city in South Africa, discussions concerning race are usually positive. Residents brag about the amazing foods and exciting festivals they enjoy mainly because of their rich ethnic mixture.

The coloured race is the majority group in Cape Town. Coloureds are a blend of black, white, and Asian bloodlines. The race was born in Cape Town. They are often called the Cape Coloureds. A religious people, they consider the church to be the center of their society. The coloureds are also known for their quick humor and fondness for entertaining. The Cape Town Minstrel Carnival, which is put on every January, is a joyful party for the whole city.

# Racial Judgments

If there were any doubt about whether a South African fit into the black or the coloured racial category, the person went to a judge for a determination. One test given was the "pencil in hair" treatment. The judge placed a pencil in the person's hair. If the pencil stood straight up, the person was classified as black. If the pencil fell to its side, the person was classified as coloured.

*Above: Students at Jan van Riebeeck Primary School*
*Below: Two Cape Coloured fishermen in Harbour Docks*

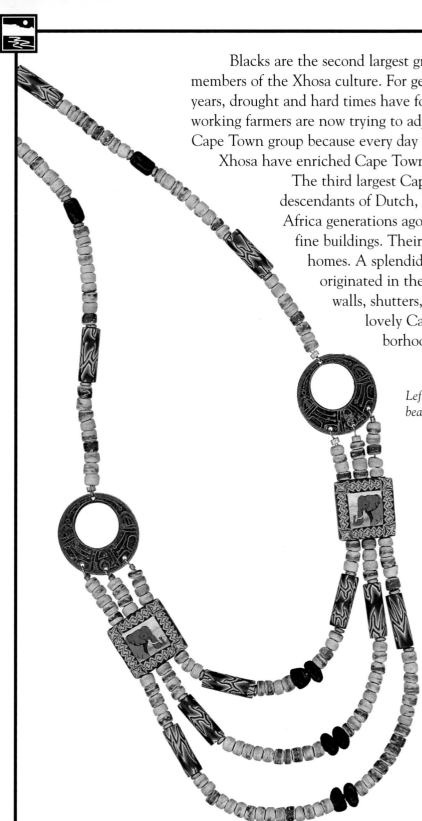

Blacks are the second largest group in Cape Town. Most Cape Town blacks are members of the Xhosa culture. For generations, the Xhosa were a rural people. In recent years, drought and hard times have forced them into the city to seek jobs. The hard-working farmers are now trying to adjust to city life. The blacks are the fastest-growing Cape Town group because every day more and more of them migrate from the farms. The Xhosa have enriched Cape Town with their music and love of art.

The third largest Cape Town ethnic group are the whites. Most are descendants of Dutch, French, and English people who came to South Africa generations ago. The whites had the skills and the money to create fine buildings. Their imprint can be seen in Cape Town's lovely older homes. A splendid form of architecture called the Cape Dutch style originated in the city. Cape Dutch houses have whitewashed outer walls, shutters, and ornamental designs over the roofs. Hundreds of lovely Cape Dutch houses stand in Cape Town's old neighborhoods and in the quaint fishing villages near the city.

*Left: An African bead necklace*

*Most Cape Town blacks are members of the Xhosa culture.*

*This old house in Stellenbosch was built in the Cape Dutch style.*

Cape Town's Asians, the fourth largest group, are often called the Cape Malay. Centuries ago, they were brought to South Africa as slaves from Malaysia in the South Pacific. Today, they live as small business owners and tradespeople. Most Malays are Muslims. Five times a day, criers call them to prayer. The call of the criers adds to the color and variety of this international city. The Malay people are also famous for running tiny restaurants that serve delicious but highly spiced food.

*A tableful of traditional highly spiced food is being served at this Malay wedding in Cape Town.*

# IMPRESSIONS OF THE CITY AND A WORD OF CAUTION

With a population of about two million, Cape Town is South Africa's second largest city. Johannesburg, to the northeast, is larger. Cape Town is South Africa's legislative capital. It is where Parliament meets. Cape Town is also the capital of Western Cape Province, perhaps the loveliest of South Africa's nine states.

Cape Town's small downtown area clings to the waterfront. A visitor can stroll from one end of downtown to the other in about half an hour. Radiating out from downtown is a sea of neighborhoods and suburbs. Outlying suburbs are usually called townships.

From a distance, the view of central Cape Town is dominated by high-rise glass-and-steel buildings. To many first-time visitors, the city seems to have an American look. But tourists walking downtown notice a pleasant European flavor. Many streets are narrow and cobblestoned. They are lined with glittering small shops. The graceful older buildings are gifts from Dutch and British architects. Clearly, the stately structures were built in an unhurried time. A particularly pleasant region is called the Company Gardens, or simply the Gardens. This was once a vegetable patch planted by early Dutch settlers. Now, it is a tree-lined park that holds notable buildings such as the South African Library.

The two young girls shown above were photographed in the Company Gardens (left), a lovely, tree-lined park in which the South African Library stands.

Not so pleasant are the townships that spread out from downtown. Many townships house black people who recently immigrated from the farms. They have positive names in the Xhosa language such as Guguletho (our pride) and Khayelitsha (our new home). However, the houses in the townships were built by immigrant families from discarded wood, scrap bricks, sheets of plastic, or even cardboard. Sewers are scarce and few streets are paved. On rainy days, residents sink up to their knees in mud. South Africa's new government guarantees political equality to all of its people. But a huge gap between rich and poor remains. Evidence of this gap is seen in the contrast between bright, lively central Cape Town and the dreariness of the townships.

The gulf between rich and poor has produced a crime problem that plagues all South African cities.

Vicious muggers, sometimes called *skolies*, roam the streets looking for people to pounce upon and rob. At times, a skolie kills a victim in the course of a robbery. Crime statistics for 1997 showed that Cape Town had passed Johannesburg to claim its dubious honor as the murder capital of South Africa. Officials insist that most of the murders are due to neighborhood feuds and gang violence. The South African tourist office assures guests that a foreigner is safe as long as he or she takes reasonable precautions.

*This mother and her son live in Spandau, one of the vast squatter camps in Cape Town where housing is even more makeshift than it is in the townships.*

Yes, street crime and poverty are ugly facts of life in Cape Town. But most tourists still hail the city as an attractive, exciting place to visit. It is the people who give the city its charm. People from all across the world have gathered here for some 350 years. And they have created the amazing city we enjoy today.

*A group of women in Spandau Squatter Camp are working with Operation Hunger in an attempt to improve life in the camp.*

*A view of Cape Town, Table Mountain, and Lion's Head*

*This Cape is the most stately thing and the fairest Cape we saw in the whole circumference of the earth.*
— English sea captain
Sir Francis Drake,
writing in 1580

Drake praised the Cape of Good Hope, which lay just south of the present-day site of Cape Town. It was here that trading ships bound from Europe to the Indies had to pass. Such voyages lasted up to two years. The Europeans decided they needed an outpost on the southern tip of Africa to service ships. For that reason, Cape Town was born.

# THE CAPE OUTPOST

I n April 1652, three Dutch sailing ships commanded by Jan van Riebeeck dropped anchor at what is today Table Bay. The ninety or so men and women aboard the vessels were ordered to build a "refreshment station," which would provide ships with vegetables, meats, and fresh water. Sponsoring the venture was the powerful Dutch East India Company. The company had grown rich by shipping tea and spices from the Indies to markets in Europe.

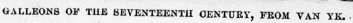

GALLEONS OF THE SEVENTEENTH CENTURY, FROM VAN YK.

*Jan van Riebeeck (above) was the commander of three Dutch sailing ships like these (left) when he dropped anchor in Table Bay in 1652.*

*A group of Zulu warriors preparing for battle with the Afrikaners*

The Dutch settlers were met by a yellow-skinned people called the Khoikhoi. They spoke in a clicking language. The Dutch nicknamed them the Hottentots (the stutterers). Though the Dutch attempted to live in peace with the local people, they still built a fort to ward off attacks. The outline of that fort can be seen today at a central Cape Town square called the Grand Parade.

Within fifty years, about 1,500 Europeans lived in the Dutch community in southern Africa. The Europeans included Dutch, Germans, and French. The Khoikhoi, who fell victim to European diseases, were beginning to disappear. Hundreds of Malayan slaves also lived in the colony. Already a new race that was darker than white but lighter than black had appeared. These people were the coloureds, now the majority group in Cape Town. Even today, the vast majority of all South Africa's coloured people live either in Cape Town or in Western Cape Province.

In 1795, Great Britain occupied Cape Town. The British had the world's largest navy. The Dutch were powerless to stop the British takeover. Old-time Dutch settlers resented British rule and journeyed to the grasslands far to the north. There, they formed a separate society, considering themselves a white tribe of Africa. In time, the Dutch called themselves Afrikaners. After arriving in the north, the Afrikaners fought a series of terrible wars with black people. The fighting stirred a mood of racial hatred that lingered over South Africa for two centuries.

*The early Dutch settlement in Cape Town*

# Cape Town and the Dawn of Human History

The Dutch settlement of 1652 marked the beginnings of Cape Town, but certainly not the start of human history in the region. In fact, southern Africa was probably the place where human beings first emerged. In 1995, three tiny footprints were discovered embedded in sandstone some 60 miles (97 kilometers) north of Cape Town. Scientists later determined the footprints were made by a woman walking on a sand dune some 117,000 years ago. These well-preserved footprints are the earliest traces of modern human beings ever found.

# THE WORLD RUSHES TO SOUTH AFRICA

Cape Town is called South Africa's "Mother City." It is where the nation began. During the 1800s, the Mother City served as a gateway to millions of Europeans who came seeking riches.

On a summer day in 1867, a Dutch boy spotted a sparkling pebble lying on the ground of his family farm north of Cape Town. A neighbor determined that the pebble was a diamond. The find sparked a stampede of European miners who came hoping to stuff their pockets with diamonds. Twenty years later, a fabulous goldfield was discovered near today's Johannesburg. Another great wave of Europeans flooded into South Africa. Most came through Cape Town, the Mother City and the nation's golden gate.

Mineral deposits helped make South Africa the richest country on the African continent. But the people suffered prolonged warfare. The British fought the Dutch. The whites fought the blacks. A sense of order finally prevailed in the early 1900s, when the Union of South Africa was formed. The Union was a self-governing country within the British Empire.

The constitution of the new country gave nearly all power to whites. Racial segregation already was a common practice through-out the Union of South Africa. In the mid-twentieth century, the subjugation of nonwhites became law under the apartheid system. The term *apartheid* comes from an Afrikaner word meaning "apartness." In English the word is pronounced ah-PAHR-tayt.

*The diamond diggings in South Africa, 1872*

*President Nelson Mandela (left) is shown at Dal Josafat Stadium (above) on the fourth anniversary of his release from prison.*

# RAINBOW CAPE TOWN

On a clear day, one can stand on Cape Town's waterfront and see Robben Island 5 miles (8 km) in the distance. The tiny island was once used as a prison colony to hold disobedient slaves. Later, it became a very special jail. Political prisoners, those who fought against apartheid, were banished to Robben Island.

One political prisoner held on Robben Island was Nelson Mandela. He was a lawyer and the son of a Xhosa chief. Because of his strong stand against the government, Mandela spent twenty-seven years in prison. For twenty of those years, he was locked up on Robben Island. Modern South Africa makes no attempt to hide its checkered past. Cape Town visitors today can take a cruise boat to Robben Island. There, guests may see the tiny cell occupied by the future South African president. There was barely room for Mandela to lie down in the cell.

Beads and woven rugs like these are among the handicrafts produced by Cape Town artisans.

Cape Town has long been a city of artists and writers. During the apartheid years, the city's artistic community was a strong voice of protest against the government's racial segregation policies. Afrikaner writer D. J. Opperman wrote a play called *Christmas Carol*, which described a coloured Christ Child born in a coloured Cape Town slum district. James Mathews, a coloured poet from Cape Town, wrote a collection of poems called *Cry Rage*.

The poems awakened such anti-apartheid passion that the South African government banned them. In one poem, Mathews contrasts the beauty of Cape Town with the ugliness of apartheid:

*It is said
that poets write of beauty
of form, of flowers and of
    love but the words I write
are of pain and rage.*

One of the saddest events of the apartheid years took place in a Cape Town mixed-race neighborhood called District Six. Lying just a few blocks east of downtown, it was a lively community of 55,000 people. Its twisting streets were filled with fruit vendors, fish sellers, and strolling musicians. The district was mostly coloured. Nevertheless, the government declared District Six to be a "white" neighborhood. Therefore, all nonwhites were ordered to move to far-flung townships. In 1966, a small army of bulldozers converged on District Six and leveled all buildings except churches and Muslim mosques. Then, for decades, the once-vibrant neighborhood lay in ruins. Only in the late 1990s were town houses built in old District Six.

Gradually, the South African government relaxed its racial segregation laws. Cape Town was a leader in the dismantling of apartheid. In 1980, Cape Town integrated its eleven city beaches. At the time, most other beaches in the nation were segregated. Shops owned by black people and coloured people opened in central Cape Town, a white district. People of all racial groups proclaimed Cape Town to be a liberal city compared to the rest of South Africa.

*This plaque is attached to St. Mark's Anglican Church in District Six, a mixed-race neighborhood that was razed by the government in 1966 and was never rebuilt.*

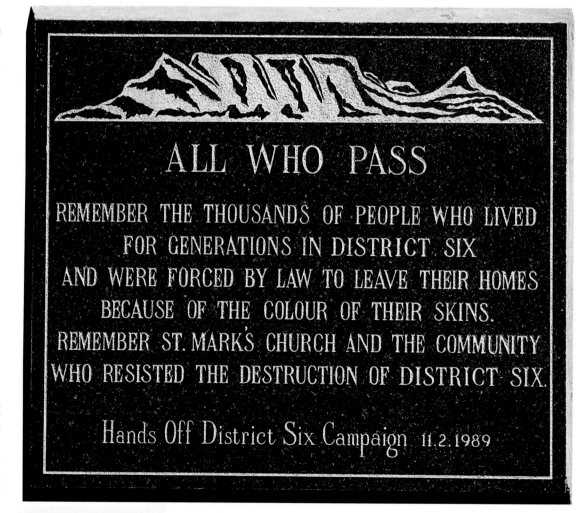

ALL WHO PASS

REMEMBER THE THOUSANDS OF PEOPLE WHO LIVED FOR GENERATIONS IN DISTRICT SIX AND WERE FORCED BY LAW TO LEAVE THEIR HOMES BECAUSE OF THE COLOUR OF THEIR SKINS. REMEMBER ST. MARK'S CHURCH AND THE COMMUNITY WHO RESISTED THE DESTRUCTION OF DISTRICT SIX.

Hands Off District Six Campaign 11.2.1989

*This is the way Cape Town's District Six looked after it was razed under a government act separating the races.*

# The District Six Museum

Memories of the charming old neighborhood are kept alive in the District Six Museum. The museum displays a map of the community and an exceptional set of photos collected from one-time residents. Also shown are District Six street signs that once hung from posts. The signs were kept by a bulldozer operator who later donated them to the museum. Elderly former residents visit the museum, see the relics of the past, and leave weeping.

*Above: Mixed-race high school students from Paarl at the fourth anniversary celebration of Nelson Mandela's release from prison.*

*Right: South Africa's president F. W. de Klerk (left) and Nelson Mandela (second from right) won the Nobel Peace Prize in 1993 for their efforts to settle the country's long-standing racial problems.*

In 1991, the government freed Nelson Mandela from his prison on Robben Island. Days after his release, Mandela made a stirring speech in front of Cape Town's old City Hall on Darling Street. Events then moved at a lightning pace. Later in 1991, the government repealed its segregation laws and ended mandatory race categories. In 1993, Mandela and South Africa's white president F. W. de Klerk jointly won the Nobel Peace Prize. They were given the prestigious award for their efforts to settle the country's long-standing racial problems peacefully. In 1994, in the nation's first free and open election, the people chose Nelson Mandela to be president of South Africa.

After Mandela's victory, a cheering crowd once more gathered in front of Cape Town's City Hall on Darling Street. It was a rainbow throng, fitting the city's profile. All hailed President Nelson Mandela. The mood was summed up by a young white woman who told a reporter, "What was so awesome about it was the sense of reconciliation and forgiveness that Mandela exhibited. . . . Some people want revenge, but he preaches love."

With the election of Mandela, apartheid officially ended. People looked forward to a new South Africa and a new and better Cape Town.

*This is the ballot marked by South Africans who voted in their country's first free and open election.*

*La la la la laa, Won't you take*
  *me home*
*La la la la laa, Back to old*
  *Cape Town*
*La la la la laa, la laa, la laa.*

This is one of the songs from *District Six: The Musical*, a show that is especially popular with the coloured people of Cape Town. The words and spirit of the musical are remarkably upbeat, though it deals with the destruction of District Six, still a bitter subject.

# GROWING UP

Cape Town children go to school, go to church, and enjoy activities with their families. Certainly, this sounds similar to the lifestyles of most North American children. But Cape Town children live with the mountains and the sea at their doorstep. Few other world cities are situated in such an exciting countryside.

Just about every Cape Town child hikes up Table Mountain. Most take the hike four or five times before they are twelve. Usually, they go with school or church groups. There are 350 recognized hiking trails up the great mountain. It takes up to three hours for a school group to make the trek to the top. The walk is exhausting, but children sing songs and giggle all the way up.

*All Cape Town children must start primary school by the age of six and continue attending school through a five-year high-school program.*

Children gasp at the view from the peak of Table Mountain. Below, houses and roads spread like anthills along the sea. Young people look for landmarks and try to find their neighborhoods in the maze. They also discover the cuddly wild animals that live on the mountain. They are dassies, or rock rabbits. About the size of house cats, dassies allow people to pet them. Though called rock rabbits, they are not really in the rabbit family. Strange as it seems, these tiny creatures are distant cousins to elephants!

Of course, a Cape Town child's life involves more than climbing Table Mountain and swimming at one of the city's many public beaches. By law, all children must start school by age six. Children attend a primary school up to the seventh grade. They then start a five-year high-school program. After high school, young men and women must pass a series of demanding tests if they wish to attend a university. The high-school drop-out rate is high, but education is a success story in the Cape Town region. Western Cape Province has South Africa's highest rate of people who can read and write.

*Many children who climb Table Mountain have a chance to pet an African rock hyrax, known as a dassie or a rock rabbit (right).*

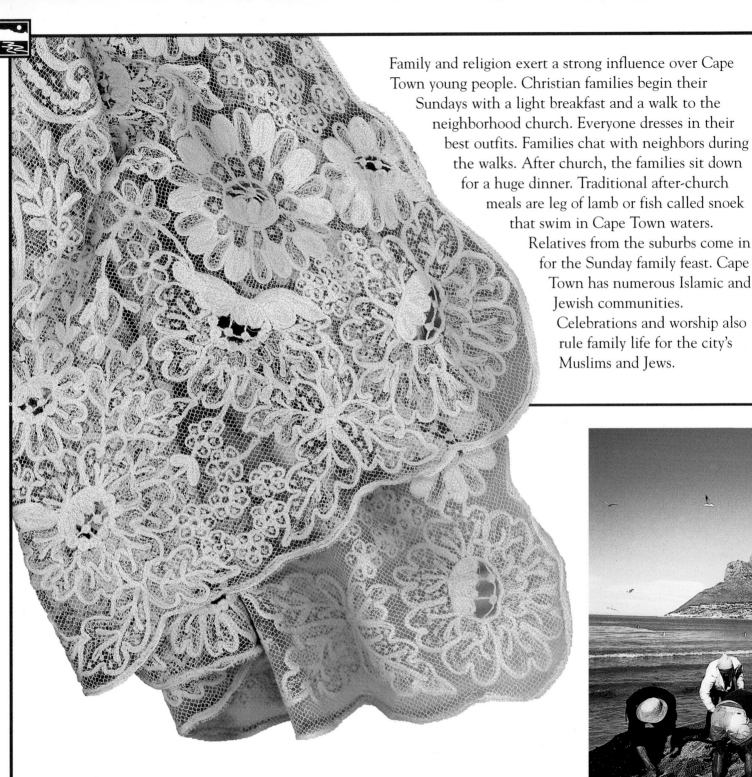

Family and religion exert a strong influence over Cape Town young people. Christian families begin their Sundays with a light breakfast and a walk to the neighborhood church. Everyone dresses in their best outfits. Families chat with neighbors during the walks. After church, the families sit down for a huge dinner. Traditional after-church meals are leg of lamb or fish called snoek that swim in Cape Town waters.

Relatives from the suburbs come in for the Sunday family feast. Cape Town has numerous Islamic and Jewish communities.

Celebrations and worship also rule family life for the city's Muslims and Jews.

*Women who dress up in their best outfits to attend church on Sunday might wear an African lace shawl like this one around their shoulders.*

# A Historic Operation

In December 1967, Dr. Christiaan Barnard of the University of Cape Town Medical School performed the first human heart transplant operation. Presiding over a thirty-person medical team, Barnard removed the healthy heart from a thirty-year-old woman who had died in an automobile crash. He placed it in the chest of a fifty-five-year-old man whose own heart was damaged by disease. Today, such heart transplants are more or less routine. However, in 1967, the worldwide medical community hailed the operation as a miracle.

*These Cape Town fishermen are catching snoek, a fish that is often served for Sunday dinner.*

Powerful influences from church and family are needed to lure kids away from gang activity. Gangs are a troubling aspect of modern Cape Town. Violent gangs rule the streets in a vast suburban area called Cape Flats. Teenaged gangs have names such as the Mongrels, the Laughing Boys, and the Scorpions. For reasons no one can explain, one Cape Flats gang is called the Young Americans. The gangs got their start years ago among children who sold newspapers or fruit and fought each other for the right to sell at busy street corners. In the old days, the clashes were limited to fistfights. Today, the gangs sell drugs and they are armed with guns. Police say gang warfare accounts for most of the city's appalling murder statistics.

# FUN IN THE RAINBOW CITY

Cape Flats is an impoverished, largely coloured area. Many families were forcibly moved there by government decree during the apartheid years. Yet the neighborhood gives Cape Town its liveliest music. Cape Coloured music features small bands made up of guitars, a drum, and singers. The bands have a curious Latin flavor. Some say slaves that were once exchanged between Brazil and South Africa brought Latin rhythms to Cape Town. Though scholars argue about the origin of Cape Colored music, no one can resist its compelling, foot-tapping beats.

*A Cape Coloured musical group performing in the Company Gardens, a popular park on the site of the first Dutch settlement*

During the long years when apartheid divided South Africa, team sports helped to bring the nation together. In Cape Town, blacks, whites, coloureds, and Asians joined integrated teams to participate in the city's favorite sport—soccer. Today, fans crowd into Cape Town's Athlone Stadium to watch the city's integrated professional soccer team, the Cape Town Spurs. Other team sports popular in Cape Town include the British imports cricket and rugby. Cricket is thought to be the ancestor of baseball, and rugby the ancestor of American-style football. Cape Town's Newlands Cricket Grounds are said to be the prettiest in the world. The city's Asians still dominate field hockey, a sport they took up years ago.

*Above: A Rugby match being played on a field overlooking the sea*

*Left: A Langa Township resident*

*Above: An Indian man selling spices in a Cape Town shop*

*Right: Boerwors, a tasty Afrikaner sausage, is sold at an outdoor snack bar in the heart of Cape Town.*

In the late 1990s, Cape Town asked the International Olympic Committee for permission to host the 2004 Olympic Games. President Nelson Mandela said, "Africa deserves a chance to host the Olympic Games in a unique African way." Teams from other countries once refused to come to South Africa for international meets because of apartheid policies. City leaders in the post-apartheid era believed the games would showcase Cape Town and create 91,000 jobs. All citizens were saddened when the committee awarded the 2004 Olympics to Athens, Greece. Hopeful residents say that someday the games will indeed come to Cape Town.

On working days, downtown sidewalks burst with energy from street vendors and entertainers. The spirited street life is a gift from Cape Town's rainbow blend of races. Black bands set up on street corners and play music that ranges from African rhythms to American jazz. Street art fairs display the creations of black artists, including sculpture and paintings that explode with color. White and coloured street vendors sell prepared food from pushcarts. A favorite street snack is a tasty Afrikaner sausage called a *boerwors*. Cape Malay performers are a hit at street fairs because of their gyrating—and dangerous-looking—sword dances. During the dances, young men flash razor-sharp swords and hurl them high in the air.

*Some Cape Town street vendors sell lengths of colorful African fabric.*

# ONE FABULOUS FESTIVAL

The granddaddy of Cape Town parties is the Cape Town Minstrel Carnival. This wild, outrageous celebration begins on New Year's Day. A dynamic party spirit takes over the town, reminding visitors from the United States of New Orleans at Mardi Gras time. Traditionally, the festival is run by coloured people, but it is enjoyed by all races.

Teams of minstrel singers take to the streets during the Cape Town Minstrel Carnival festivities. They wear loud sport coats of yellow and flaming pink. Teams keep their "uniforms" secret until the morning they put them on. There are many minstrel bands, and no one wants their special sport coats to be copied by others. On the streets, the minstrel groups sing *moppies*, lively little songs. Each tiny band also has a banjo player, a drummer, and a flute or whistle player.

The last act in this noisy drama comes with a grand parade of all the

## An Outdoor City

Cape Town's weather has been compared to the gentle Mediterranean climate of southern Italy and Greece. Rarely is it shivering cold or uncomfortably hot and humid. Long sunny days encourage outdoor living. For that reason, festivals are held on the streets. New Year's Day, when the Cape Town Minstrel Carnival is held, comes at an especially pleasant time. Cape Town is in the Southern Hemisphere. Its winter season arrives in July and August. Sometimes, cold rainy days prevail in the winter months. Also, powerful winds called "Cape Doctors" can blow in from the sea.

*Left and right: Participants in the annual New Year's Cape Town Minstrel Carnival*

minstrel teams down the main streets of Cape Town. Spectators line the sidewalks to watch the bands sing and play while they march. The parade ends at Cape Town's Green Point Stadium. There, judging takes place. First place goes to the most creative and vibrant minstrel team. Competition is fierce. But when judgment is passed, the losers celebrate with the winners.

Cape Town celebrates other festivals. Christmas is a time of lights and carol singing. During the summer months, outdoor concerts are held at the Kirstenbosch Botanical Gardens. Several wine festivals highlight April and May. Still, nothing overshadows the Cape Town Minstrel Carnival. It is the city's New Year's bash.

*Holiday candles*

# CAPE"

Cape Town was once called the "Tavern by the Sea." It was so named by sailors who enjoyed pulling into the port for a good meal and a good time after a long voyage. Ships' captains used to give a silver coin to the first sailor to spot Table Mountain. On clear days, the majestic mountain can be seen 100 miles (161 km) out to sea. Most modern visitors arrive by air. No matter how one arrives, the town still excites guests by giving them plenty of things to do and sights to see.

# CENTRAL CAPE TOWN

Central Cape Town is the city's historic heart. Here, a tiny band of Dutch people established an outpost that grew into a modern city. Tourists visiting the central region stop first at the Castle of Good Hope. Built in 1666, it is South Africa's oldest structure. The castle rises over the original site of the fort erected by van Riebeeck and his Dutch settlers.

Inside the castle are several museums and paintings of Cape Town as it looked hundreds of years ago.

Nearby, is the Koopmans de Wet House. Now a museum, the house was built in 1701 and contains splendid examples of Cape furniture and silver items. Another memorable building in central Cape Town is the 1841 Groote Kerk (Dutch words meaning "Great Church").

Among the interesting features of the Groote Kerk are its pews, each with its own door and key. Wealthy families could lock the pew door and not be forced to worship with the masses. Outside the church, a sign marks the Slave Tree. Under this towering old pine tree, slaves were auctioned and sold to the highest bidder.

Many of the slaves brought to South Africa came from Indonesia and Malaysia in the far Pacific. Today, the Malay district, called Bo-Kaap, is one of Central Cape Town's most interesting neighborhoods. The smell of curry wafts through doorways of restaurants here. Prayers are chanted inside mosques. Men wear a brimless cap called a fez.

*The Castle of Good Hope, built in 1666, is South Africa's oldest structure.*

A red fez means the wearer has completed a pilgrimage to the holy city of Mecca in Saudi Arabia. Cape Malay people have lived in this neighborhood for hundreds of years. The Bo-Kaap Museum details their contributions to Cape Town.

*Above: The Bo-Kaap Malay district of Cape Town*

*Left: This young man is wearing a red fez, which means he has completed a pilgrimage to Mecca.*

A pleasant walk awaits people in a parklike area called the Company Gardens. Hundreds of years ago, Dutch settlers raised cabbages, carrots, and potatoes here to sell to passing ships. Today, the gardens consist of tree-lined walkways leading to museums and government buildings. The trees and shrubs come from all over the world: firewood trees from Australia, magnolias from Texas, and hat palms from Puerto Rico.

Cape Town's most popular museums are found in or near the Company Gardens. The South African Museum, the country's oldest, contains fossils of dinosaurs and skeletons of whales. The building housing the South African Cultural Museum started out in 1679 as slave quarters. Today, the South African Cultural Museum displays coins, furniture, and artworks that detail the nation's various ethnic groups. The South African National Gallery shows paintings by Europeans as well as works of art by

Xhosa and Zulu masters. Irma Stern, who died in 1966, was perhaps South Africa's finest painter. Her paintings are displayed at the Irma Stern Museum. The Jewish Museum is housed in a synagogue built in 1841. It traces the history of Cape Town's Jewish community.

*The South African Museum (above) is the oldest museum in the country.*

# Cecil Rhodes, Diamond King and Builder

Towering over the Company Gardens is a statue of the amazing Englishman Cecil Rhodes. He came to South Africa as a seventeen-year-old in 1870. Rhodes gained control of diamond mines and became one of the world's richest men. With his fortune, he planned to build a railroad running north from Cape Town to the city of Cairo in Egypt. He died before this ambitious project could get underway. His memory lives in the Rhodes Scholarships that are awarded to deserving college students from all over the world. The statue in the Gardens shows Cecil Rhodes pointing north. The inscription below tells South Africans, "Your hinterland is there."

*A fountain and pond in the Company Gardens*

# THE VICTORIA AND ALFRED WATERFRONT

Cape Town has many old landmark buildings that display its history. It also has shopping centers and towering office buildings that make it as modern as tomorrow. The city's ultramodern section is the Victoria and Alfred Waterfront. The waterfront is a downtown neighborhood created in recent years by dumping landfill into the bay. It was named after Great Britain's Queen Victoria and her son Alfred. Today, it is Cape Town's busiest tourist section. The Victoria and Alfred Waterfront is crammed with restaurants, theaters, and craft shops.

The waterfront's latest attraction is the Two Oceans Aquarium. Marine life from the Indian and the Atlantic Oceans is on display at the aquarium. The Maritime Museum traces the history of ships from prehistoric times. Cruise boats take visitors on scenic trips along the Victoria and Alfred Waterfront. One cruise boat that has been in use for years is still called the "Penny Ferry." Today, it costs far more than a penny to ride the ferry.

The Victoria and Alfred Waterfront neatly combines tourist pleasures with a working harbor. Cape Town is a busy commercial seaport. Huge freighters unload cargo near docks where pleasure boats bob at

*A woven straw basket with an African design*

*The Victoria and Alfred Waterfront at night*

anchor. But the cargo docks are situated in such a way that strollers or those dining at waterfront restaurants hardly notice the crews unloading huge ships.

Not far from the waterfront is Sea Point, a suburb that contains some of Cape Town's richest housing. It is said that Sea Point never sleeps. Its trendy restaurants and nightclubs are busy at all hours. Signal Hill rises nearby. On the top of this hill stands a cannon, the Noon Gun. It is fired at twelve noon every day except Sunday. Years ago, the cannon was used to inform ship captains of the precise time so they could set their clocks. Now, in the days of digital timepieces, the cannon does little more than frighten the city's flocks of pigeons. The noonday blasts continue only because they are a Cape Town tradition.

*The new Victoria Wharf complex is crammed with restaurants, craft shops, and theaters.*

# THE CAPE PENINSULA

Stretching 25 miles (40 km) south of Cape Town is the scenic Cape Peninsula. It is a narrow stem of land containing rocky mountains, pristine beaches, quaint fishing villages, and wildlife habitats. No visit to Cape Town is complete without a tour of the stunning Cape Peninsula.

Camps Bay is a favorite beach for swimmers and sunbathers. But the waters here can be frigid even in South Africa's summer months. To the rear of the beach, hiking trails lead up to a mountain formation called Lion's Head, so named because it looks like one. Also on the peninsula is the 1,300-acre (526-hectare) Kirstenbosch National Botanic Gardens. This wonderful area is on land once owned by the tycoon Cecil Rhodes. The garden contains more than 4,000 flowers and plants typical of the South African region.

*Camps Bay, on the Cape Peninsula, is a favorite beach for swimmers and sunbathers.*

*Above: Plantings in the Kirstenbosch National Botanic Garden*
*Right: A newly molted jackass penguin on the Cape Peninsula*

Even close to the big city, wildlife runs free on the Cape Peninsula. Look to the shore and you might see a school of humpback whales bursting through the waves. Pelicans, gulls, and sunbirds skim over the surf. Take a hike along the rocks and perhaps you will encounter groups of superbly comical penguins strutting about. They belong to a unique species called the jackass penguin.

## Just Nuisance

The port of Simon's Town has been a naval base for nearly 200 years. During World War II, many British warships stopped here. Weary sailors were greeted by an old friend, an enormous Great Dane that lived on the base. The dog loved attention. He nudged his huge head into the laps of sailors to demand petting. So the sailors named him, affectionately, Just Nuisance. When Just Nuisance died, the British navy gave him a full military funeral with a band and an honor guard. His bronze statue now stands in the center of Simon's Town.

Some visitors on the Cape Peninsula close their eyes and try to imagine a famous ghost ship. It is said that a ship commanded by the Dutch captain Van der Decken was caught in a violent storm here in 1641. With his ship sinking fast, Van der Decken shouted to the skies that he would reach his home port even if it took forever. Perhaps he sank. Perhaps. Van der Decken's voyage was immortalized in the Legend of the Flying Dutchman. Over the centuries, sailors and people on land claim to have seen the Flying Dutchman's ghost ship off the Cape Peninsula. The ship appears most frequently during storms. Be careful if you see it. The legend also says that anyone catching a glimpse of the Flying Dutchman is doomed.

The Cape of Good Hope Nature Reserve covers the southern third of Cape Peninsula. Covering almost 20,000 acres (8,094 ha), the reserve is home to antelope, zebra, fox, and more than 160 species of birds. It is also home to some unusual baboons. They are unique in that they feed on the marine life they find on beaches at low tide.

*Wooden African animals like the ones shown on this page can be purchased in many Cape Town shops.*

*South African antelopes called bonteboks inhabit the Cape of Good Hope Nature Reserve.*

*This spectacular view of Cape Town was taken from the top of Table Mouontain.*

Over the years, baboons in the Cape of Good Hope Nature Reserve have also accepted food from tourists, and herein lies a grave problem. Frequently, the baboons pounce on a car or a tour bus and scratch on the windows demanding handouts. Don't feed them! These baboons have vice-like jaws and can bite you down to the bone.

The return trip to Cape Town means a drive toward Table Mountain. Many tourists begin and end a visit to the city by taking the cable-car ride to the top. The ride, taken in a swaying car, is almost as scary as a roller coaster. However, the cable car was installed in 1929 and has never had an accident. Visitors notice that the top of Table Mountain has rocky hills and crevasses. Its remarkable flatness as seen from the ground is an illusion created by height and distance. The view from the peak is breathtak-ing. Below, the sea seems to kiss the shoreline of Cape Town, one of the world's most inviting cities.

# FAMOUS LANDMARKS

Table Mountain and Lion's Head

Victoria and Alfred Waterfront

### Table Mountain
This great flat-topped mountain can be seen from anywhere in Cape Town and up to 100 miles (161 km) out to sea. Cape Town residents call it "our mountain."

### The Royal Cape Yacht Club
On the city's waterfront, the yacht club provides year-round accommodations for luxurious yachts. It is also the starting point for the Race to Rio, a dash across the South Atlantic that attracts the world's best yachts and crews.

### Victoria and Alfred Waterfront
A neighborhood of theaters and fine restaurants, the Victoria and Alfred Waterfront is Cape Town's biggest tourist draw.

### The Two Oceans Aquarium and the South African Maritime Museum
Both museums are recent additions to the Victoria and Alfred Waterfront neighborhood.

### Golden Acres
A huge office and shopping complex, Golden Acres accents the modern aspects of Cape Town.

### The Castle of Good Hope
Built in 1666, largely with the help of slave labor, the Castle of Good Hope is Cape Town's oldest structure.

### Adderley Street
Cape Town's main thoroughfare, Adderley Street is lined with high-rise buildings. On the street's central island are palm trees, fountains, and impressive statues.

### Company Gardens
Stretching along upper Adderley Street is a leafy section called Company Gardens where Dutch settlers once grew vegetables to sell to ships. Within the gardens are a sundial dating from 1787 and a bell tower made in 1855.

Clifton Beach at sunset

House of Parliament

The Two Oceans Aquarium

**Grand Parade**
One of Cape Town's historic squares, it once served as a military parade ground. Thick red lines drawn on the square's grounds indicate where the original Dutch fort once stood.

**House of Parliament**
It was in Cape Town's parliament building that the controversial apartheid laws were made and later unmade. Visitors may sit in the galleries and watch today's mixed-race parliament at work.

**Clifton**
With four public beaches, this section of the Cape Peninsula is Cape Town's favorite summer getaway spot.

**Hout Bay**
A Cape Peninsula resort village that fronts the sea and has Table Mountain as a backdrop, Hout Bay is also famous for its many craft stores.

**Fish Hoek**
This seaside Cape Peninsula town features a windswept beach with clear waters that are especially popular with scuba divers.

**Rietvlei Nature Reserve**
Containing one of the Cape Peninsula's few lakes, this reserve is home to a wide variety of birds.

**Cape of Good Hope Nature Reserve**
On the southern tip of the Cape Peninsula, the Cape of Good Hope Nature Reserve is home to baboons, zebras, and many other animals.

# FAST FACTS

## POPULATION

City: 789,580
Metropolitan Area: 2,000,000

## AREA

116 square miles (300 sq km)

## CLIMATE

Cape Town enjoys a "Mediterranean climate" similar to that of Italy and Greece. Visitors need not bring special clothes to Cape Town regardless of what time of year they come. Even in winter, between June and August, temperatures range between 45 degrees Fahrenheit (7° Celsius) and 65 degrees Fahrenheit (18° Celsius). Summers, between December and March, are warm and pleasant, not uncomfortably hot and humid. The average summer temperature is 79 degrees Fahrenheit (26° Celsius). Rain falls mainly in the winter months.

## INDUSTRIES

Shipping is Cape Town's traditional industry, and the city remains a busy port. The city's dry docks, where ships are repaired, are the biggest in Africa. Factories in Cape Town produce clothing, shoes, chemicals, automobiles, and metal products. Tourism is a prime source of jobs. Many Cape Town residents are government employees. South Africa claims three capital cities: Cape Town is the legislative capital (where Parliament meets), Pretoria is the administrative capital, and Bloemfontein is the judicial capital.

## TRANSPORTATION

Most visitors arrive by air at Cape Town International Airport. The airport is about 14 miles (22 km) from the city center. Trains run from Cape Town's main station (in the heart of downtown) to just about every large city in South Africa. The famous Blue Train runs from Cape Town to Johannesburg, a 25-hour trip. The Blue Train has luxury cabins and first-class dining. Within the city, people ride buses and taxicabs. There is no subway system.

# CHRONOLOGY

**100,000 B.C.**
Early human beings live in the Cape Town region; footprints of a prehistoric woman were recently discovered embedded in sandstone outside of Cape Town.

**8000 B.C.**
Hunting people live throughout South Africa.

**A.D. 1488**
Portuguese sailors are the first Europeans to round the Cape of Good Hope.

**1652**
Dutch settlers establish a "refreshment station" at the site of Cape Town.

**1657**
Slaves are brought to the Cape Town outpost from Indonesia and Malaysia.

**1700**
As many as 1,500 Europeans live at the outpost that becomes Cape Town.

**1795**
The powerful British navy takes over Cape Town.

**1867**
Diamonds are discovered in farmland far north of Cape Town.

**1886**
A fabulous goldfield is found at present-day Johannesburg.

**1899–1902**
The British defeat the Dutch farmers (called Boers) in the Second Boer War.

**1910**
Union of South Africa is formed, making South Africa a self-governing country within the British Empire.

*A downtown Cape Town
street near the Victoria Hotel*

**1948**
The National Party comes to power in South Africa and legalizes racial segregation under a policy called apartheid.

**1962**
Anti-apartheid leader Nelson Mandela is arrested; he is later sentenced to life in prison.

**1966**
Bulldozers tear down a once-vibrant Cape Town neighborhood called District Six; the neighborhood was coloured, but the government declared it to be white under the Apartheid Group Area Laws.

**1980**
Cape Town integrates its beaches while beaches in most of South Africa remain segregated.

**1991**
Nelson Mandela is released from prison at Robben Island.

**1993**
Nelson Mandela and South African president F. W. de Klerk jointly win the Nobel Peace Prize.

**1994**
In the nation's first election open to all people, Nelson Mandela becomes president of South Africa.

**1997**
The International Olympic Committee turns down Cape Town's bid to host the 2004 games, and gives them instead to Athens.

# CAPE TOWN

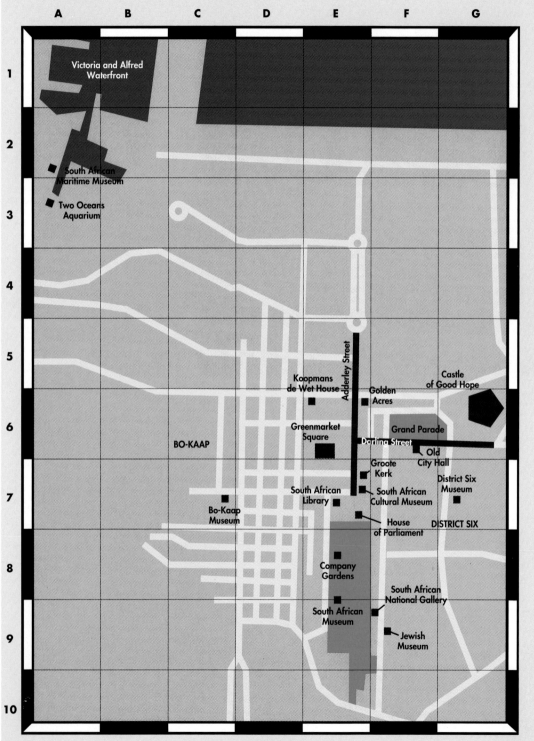

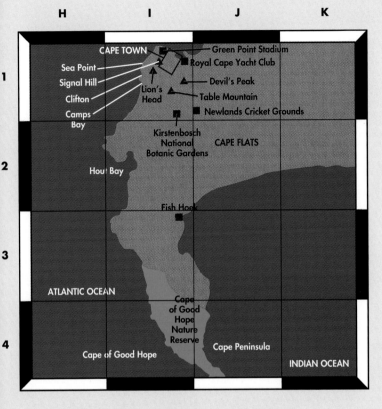

## CAPE TOWN AND SURROUNDINGS

# GLOSSARY

**apartheid:** The series of laws that governed South Africa in the past and enforced racial segregation

**decree:** A law

**dubious:** Doubtful

**ethnic:** Relating to a group based on race or nationality

**gyrating:** Pulsating or spinning

**majestic:** Dignified, inspiring

**mosque:** A house of worship for Muslims

**pristine:** Especially clean, untouched

**subjugation:** Oppression or domination

**turbulent:** Restless or violent

**waft:** To float or move lightly

## Picture Identifications

**Cover:** A view of the South African Museum and Table Mountain, the new South Africa flag, schoolgirls in Cape Province
**Page 1:** Schoolchildren with new South Africa flags on the steps of Parliament
**Pages 4–5:** Cloud over Table Mountain
**Pages 8–9:** A couple in Rust-En-Vrede wine cellars, Cape Town
**Pages 20–21:** Cape of Good Hope, Cape Town area
**Pages 32–33:** Children in the fishing village of Kassiesbaai, Cape region
**Pages 44–45:** The revitalized Victoria and Alfred Waterfront

# INDEX

*Page numbers in boldface type indicate illustrations*

# TO FIND OUT MORE

## BOOKS

Bradley, Catherine. *Causes and Consequences of the End of Apartheid.* Austin, Texas: Raintree Steck-Vaughn, 1995.

Case, Dianne. *92 Queens Road.* New York: Farrar, Staus & Giroux, 1995. Grade 6-10 novel based on author's experiences growing up coloured in Cape Town during the 1960s.

Cooper, Floyd. *Mandela: From the Life of the South African Statesman.* New York: Philomel Books, 1996.

Feinberg, Brian. *Nelson Mandela.* Junior World Biographies series. New York: Chelsea House Publishing, 1996.

Flint, David. *South Africa.* Modern Industrial World series. Thomson Learning, 1996.

Gibson, Glenda Anne (ed.). *Picture Cape Town: Landmarks of a New Generation.* Los Angeles: Getty Center for Education in the Arts, 1997.

Joyce, Peter. *Cape Town.* Globetrotters Travel Guide series. Old Saybrook, Conn.: Globe Pequot Press, 1996.

Smith, Chris. *Conflict in Southern Africa.* Parsippany, N.J.: New Discovery, 1993.

## ONLINE SITES

**Africa Books**
http://www.twooceans.co.za/Bookshop/africa.shtml
Excerpts, some quite extensive, from current books on Africa, including *Best of African Wildlife, Cape Town (the Argus), Hotels, South Africa on a Budget,* and more. One of the most extensive and beautiful selections is *Journey through South Africa* (see separate entry)

**Cape Connection**
http://www.capeconnection.co.za
A source of information about Cape Town and the Western Cape, its people, and their activities. Many links to area tourist destinations, government and business news, art, theater, music, restaurants, annual events, and much more.

**Cape Town South Africa**
http://www.ctcc.gov.za/
The official Cape Town tourism and business information home page with links to tourism; general information; a site map that links to information on arts, culture, entertainment, galleries, theater, music, festivals, museums, music, arts & crafts, restaurants, antiques, major attractions; and a pictorial tour (click on the map to take the tour)

**Journey through South Africa**
http://www.twooceans.co.za/Bookshop/africa.shtml
The book by Gerald Cubitt (photographs) and Peter Joyce (text) takes you on an extensive journey through South Africa; includes information on the land; the people; the main cities including Cape Town, Durban, Pretoria, and Johannesburg; game parks and nature reserves; all are illustrated with excellent photography and include links to other sites

**Junior NetNews, South Africa**
http://www.liber.se/aw/eng/junior_netnews/nrl_ht_97/southafr.html
An overview of South Africa, including a section on Cape Town and a picture of Table Mountain with its "tablecloth."

**Welcome to Cape Town!**
http://www.africa.com/captour/guide/welcome.htm
An overview of the Mother City and its peninsula with a link to the Western Cape Guide.

**Western Cape Travel & Tourism**
http://www.southafrica.net/tourism/wcape.html
A view of the Western Cape with links to Cape Town (including a map), museums, art galleries, monuments, shopping, nightlife, travel tips, major annual events, scheduled tours, and travel information.

## ABOUT THE AUTHOR

R. Conrad Stein was born and grew up in Chicago. After serving in the U.S. Marine Corps, he attended the University of Illinois where he earned a degree in history. He later earned an advanced degree at the University of Guanajuato in Mexico. Mr. Stein is a full-time writer of books for young readers, with more than eighty titles published. He lives in Chicago with his wife and their daughter, Janna.

Several years ago, Mr. Stein traveled to South Africa to research a book he wrote on the country for Children's Press. He found South Africa to be beautiful and the people to be friendly. Far and away the highlight of his tour was a lengthy visit to Cape Town—South Africa's wonderful Mother City.